Thigmotropism

By
Lee Pennington

Books by Lee Pennington

The Dark Hills of Jesse Stuart (criticism), 1967.
Scenes from a Southern Road (poetry), 1969.
Poems and Prints (poetry), 1969.
Wildflower...Poems for Joy (poetry), 1970.
April Poems (poetry), 1971.
Appalachia, My Sorrow (drama), 1971.
Songs of Bloody Harlan (poetry), 1975.
Spring of Violets (poetry), 1976.
Coalmine (drama), 1976.
The Porch (drama), 1976.
The Spirit of Poor Fork (drama), 1976.
Creative Composition (textbook), 1976.
I Knew a Woman (poetry), 1977.
Ragweed (drama), 1980.
The Janus Collection (poetry/photography), 1982.
Foxwind (drama), 1984.
Appalachian Quartet (drama), 1984.
The Scotian Women (drama), 1984.
Thigmotropism (poetry), 1993.

For Joy

Acknowledgments: Appreciation to publications
where certain of these poems first appeared—*Jefferson
Review, Lifestyle Magazine, Pegasus, Poet* (India).

ISBN   0-9623666-3-3 (cloth)
        0-9623666-4-1 (paper)

First Edition

Designer: Ben Ruiz

PRINTED IN THE UNITED STATES OF AMERICA

Green River Writers/Grex Press
Louisville, Kentucky

"A climbing plant which needs a prop will creep toward the nearest support. Should this be shifted, the vine, within a few hours, will change its course into the new direction. Can the plant see the pole? Does it sense it in some unfathomed way? If a plant is growing between obstructions and cannot see a potential support it will unerringly grow toward a hidden support, avoiding the area where none exists." [1]

[1]Excerpt from *THE SECRET LIFE OF PLANTS* by Peter Tompkins and Christopher Bird. Copyright ©1973 by Peter Tompkins and Christopher Bird. Reprinted by permission of HarperCollins Publishers Inc.

Contents

Part III
To Wake a World

Part IV
Circles

Part I

Lost and Found

1

Lost and Found

If you look for me, you will find me
in the center of dog howls or the needle's
eyes of sirens ripping across cities lost,
or beside night's face gaunt as strangers'
stares and empty hands flung against the sky.

If you look for me, consider the wind whispers
haunting each season's hold—a pruning of
love's limbs and briar thorns, roses
entanglement, the light's sharp pointed
rays separating darkness of each sound.

If you find me, you will no longer
be able to speak; it's the other side
of a hidden universe, the soul of ice
for I dwell where bushes burn
and once found there is no return.

3

Who Are You?

Who are you? she asked and for
nearly a hundred hours I've tried
to say it right. Something akin
I've thought to starlight and shadows,
water and earth, sky and wind, sound
and silence, all and neither.
The line where one ends and the other
begins. The way a leaf spills out
from a tree, green filling space
not yet occupied yet in that
place always having been I am.
I cannot tell my hands from love
nor my eyes from wings that have
walked with the gods mistaken
for a man and among men mistaken
for a god. Like blowing away flame,
being neither fire nor stem,
I am the moment between, the silence
that hangs on the blue edge
of every whisper. I have been
both rainbow and storm and
my total worth is
a universe beginning.

You Can

You can follow me any dew wet
morning zig-zagging across the lawn,
and see what I see—the night
rubbed like cat hair backwards
till sparks of dawn light the mind
like fireflies. You can even think
some of the thoughts I have coffee
brown and soaked feet and places
shaped like an hour glass, time's warning.
I fill my pockets with shadows
and tuck rays of sun under my shirt.
It's just a blessing to be, walking this way,
quiet as a rabbit, slinking like a wolf
waving half the wings of dragon flies.
I have been this way since I can remember.
I have no argument with silver backed glass.
Hours I've stood, knowing better, waiting for wind
to play orange trumpets down in the grass.

Hidden Roots

In a manner of speaking I guess I've grown
too philosophical, having watched all birds
fly and grass brown down to hidden roots.
Much to regret there is not more one
can say, light a flimsy excuse for any day,
and dark no particular reason for the night.
Still at the edge of any pounding sea
green hair special to coral rocks
pretends itself earth's mysterious mistress
open to foamy waves, love tides
and the swishing virginal breaking, that ritual
practices on every whisper edge of fish songs.

Concealed

Wading the lawn wet and shadowy
to watch grass eyes catch the light,
I have been known to hide
hour on hour, common as a bush,
part of a microcosm, this universe,
so much so that early rising neighbors
no longer think it strange, no longer wave
else they be suspected of greeting a tree.

There with the wind and leaves greening
I make sounds subtle as a bird,
such singing now accepted natural as the dawn,
and so concealed, fitting like bark,
no like roots, I hold to the truth
of every morning, sad rays blinding dew
clear as blood on the crucifix of limbs.

And a dragging monk's robe, dark
as time just gone, capillaries the damp
to my knees, a way of fitting in
I say with no listeners, a way to give
sound to that tree falling in the distant forest.

There but for the path wet shoes make
and the sweep of cloth to widen it,
no one would ever know and even then
they accept it as dark fingers stretched
into winding shadows, never realizing
the sun burns away where I've been.

In such acceptance I am merely part
of the foliage, the grass, the earth
simply one more secret, the answer
to another question no one bothered to ask.

I Hold To Fire

I hold to fire though the burning burn,
fingers themselves wood, dark tentacles
that weigh heart in smoke and hiss, and turn
every eye mirror into sight that pulls
a dream vision torn. I clutch to flames
a will not quite my own, nor some other
but in between—a claim of ash, a name
breath lifted grey, smoke shadows smother
which the far reaches of love having burned.
Rising as I would this bond of light
over dark at times enchanted learned
not the first flicker leap I am despite
dreadful heat the strike readying burst.
I cling as if such choice were my own—
something of bush, holy heat and bone
a consummation of flesh and thirst.

I Hold This

In the quiet of morning
I hold this truth:
night is a heavy thing,
a fat hobo, uncouth
who travels boxcars
the mind tries to hide—
a question never asked
an answer never replied.
On such rails I have
been myself a sultry thing
brother to what darkness conceals
those careful songs that flowers sing.

Bloodrush

The awesome weight—one eighty moons—
might break an ordinary heart.
But yours not that, not common
nor frail but bold, a grip of granite
on life's invariables. Not since
the sun has any dawn held fast
the rich morning fog, the rope
to bind wolves howling distant ways,
far away night bright as familiar look.
Thus, I hold you willingly leaf and vein,
a bloodrush of love, pale
tassels feeding grains
remembrance incredible as corn.

In the Moon of Making

In the Moon of Making Fat, day twenty-
three, I claim a peace with the heart's
universe, love's swirling planets and comet
tails, and cosmic dust the stuff of bones,
near distant thinking exploding suns.
I have been reading the clouds,
earth words, more than faces
and gods and animals large and wild,
there is something in the silence,
something said, and I am glad
beyond the floating fluff and light where
stars fill up the night with shapes
the myth of dreams. My hands fling
secretly outward, two fish in white
water, homing back to mystery distant
from dawn sea. In the Moon of Memory—I,
brother to the earth, lover to the sky.

In the Blue of My Morning

In the blue of my morning
cloud north of dark, south of stone,
in the middle of sand dreams
I wake hearing songs of leaves
the green whispers against the stillness
and after the waterfall of love
where prism rainbows circle
the whole of my thoughts, I wrap
all worth memory holding—
the color of your eyes at dawn,
your hair wet from rain,
the way your body curves with the earth,
the sound of leaves breaking under us,
your hands searching
laughter turned loose on eternity—
and I am blind with wisdom far
too rich to tell, yet say it somehow
in the blue of my morning, here, now—
everything I dream, I see; everything
I see, I touch; everything I touch,
I become, even now, even here,
even this.

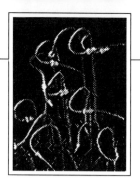

Part II

Weightier Than Love

Weightier Than Love

There are things weightier than love.
Take, for example, contrived indifference
and justice balance to throw the gold
askew or the stopped hands of clocks
with no rushed madness to dawn,
tied and howling dogs afraid of hot air
balloons, a wreckless whisper frosty white
over winter drawn. Even truth
with its little rosy smile and clapping hand
walks on crutches, leaves wheelchair tracks in snow.
Love is no more than a wet spot
awakened in some far off memory
a June bug's leg, a scarab
happy with his roll. You can
carry a whole sack full in
your eyes and not hear any bones.

Pliocene Silence

I have fondled the distant silence
like soft whispers breathed away
by a river wind, held the burden
frost against coming green,
and stones of a lost cave
fragile as immortality rest in my
thoughts like Pliocene reptile eggs.
Frogs in a far away youth sing a dirge
I've forgotten to remember. Lines
in my hands go blank in the light.
I have dreamed the beast of love,
this flower apparition in some spring,
and held to listening as if the quiet
will break like birds against glass
where only water, earth's lover,
is left to sing.

Morning Turns

The morning turns its bone like a cheek
against trees and shadows chase rabbits
across the lawn clover blossom high white dewy
eyes. Gnats fly formation over a spot of sun
filtering down through silent limbs, an imaginary
bright face on the grass. Late in the lips
of clouds a new season comes, in the middle
of the Moon when Cherries turn Black,
birds, restless, sing a summer gone
and the first dance of downing leaves is soon.
The time of spiders and great grey
traps spread everywhere that praying mantis poise
camouflaged on green flower stems. Cicadas claim
Pharaoh's bondage crushed, ignore coming frost.
Tomorrow's edges break away like laughter, like glass,
where moon blood is lost.

19

In the Pretty Flower Wind
of Morning

In the pretty flower wind of morning
the sun slips beside rabbits eating
clover blossoms, moves quiet as
a shadow's lover dawn to
the edge of the street, turns right
on Daisy and along the grey
to the main artery where cars,
a pack of tired dogs, chase
some invisible fox, chase something.

Birds tell it like limbs, like leaves,
sing at the north edge of the day's heat
and the weight of the pumpkin hanging
in the lilac bush makes the earth
closer each day, seed gone seeds mocking
return to the first dark growing,
a womb of sorts if love be such longing.

Quiet empty mailboxes guard the road
like old Romans gone to sleep, here where
no one save the sun walks, not at this
hour, at this place. It is now the
dominion of late July magnolia blossom,
queens of the sweet air lifting their white
dresses and Mary's gold on the day's ringfinger
and glads—peach, yellow and red—opening.

20

It would be enough, but there's always more,
to affirm the great dawn yes, to say
I have walked barefoot on a path
brick laid with bird songs, squares held tight
with straws cooled by the dew, but
between the watch, the wait, there is still
the day and beyond that the night to contend with.

So in the pretty flower wind morning
I watch the black cat stalk
and later find scattered everywhere
feathers south of silence.

A Special Dark

Inside you is a special dark
clinging to wet walls
thick as love
and no sun, no shine
except the hearts blood
except thoughts thrust
can sense the dream, feel that awesome stream.

And knowledge desperate as breath
tied on tips of snake forked tongues
in peach seeds carried and buried by squirrels
the feeders can walk on water
bumblebees, aerodynamic wrecks, can fly
lizards grow new tails
hog serpents a thousand times die
seeds hidden under any rock come to light.

Having been before my own sun
breaking Agamemnon
feeling grass green startle gravel drives
or pavement cracks,
there is night the roots know
sought by every raindrop down
where sap at last finds the sky.

Angels

Pigeons swirl through blue wake of cold,
four below six feet up against the clapboard wall,
perhaps colder across the knuckle ground,
yet no sign of spring nor frosty swell.

Against a sky higher than a moment's dream
fourteen dark angel figures sweep the wind,
space as silent as huddled smoke, no sound
this distance anyone can tell.

How then such indelible wings mark the place
concentrically above bricks and darkly limb
and smoke with icy eyes stares blankly
winter young at worlds already old.

Wish

You need not hold the pale night
against your whisper face
nor trust some wind blowing by
to wake the sleeping grass.

You need not wish the falling stars
out of darkened space;
their burning trails wide as love
leave such great emptiness.

Songs Still Waiting

Forgive, love, the silence—now like a banjo
empty of strings and songs still waiting in soft
wanting sun. Rains come new but not here,
not trapped in the glass free prison where we are.
If I be silent, it's because my heart fingers
speak too much. As eyes have no reason
save to look and ears to hear, my bones
know wisdom beyond even hope. Have you,
by the way, watched morning come? Did
you expect the dark to have eternal hold?
I lift a thought like wings above your hair.
Time is, after all, at once foe and friend and all
we claim of each other's needs and notions.
Warped rings will not roll so well unless
the floor match precisely the silver's bend. Then,
too, silence is little more than all the world's noises
quiet and violets purpling up the light.

Patient Escape

Beneath the flowers of your fingers
hides a root startled blind
where no sun escaped its chamber
no witness light nor warming kind;
yet find that flesh with perfect nails
to point to touch to reach beyond
mere fire unleashed, unconsumed,
the patient escape of blonde
ripe hay, furrowed fields, lines
eternity's link where glass and gold
rings hold passion still, silent
as all the songs of old.
Blooming, then, of love and life
colors imagine their own awakening
and that grand old figure, scythe
in hand, mocks with his beckoning.

The Skies Speak Snow

The skies speak snow a limb-bow's length
from winter, softly with the patience
of noise, there where grey holds
something invisible. White spiders
grow, find distance without gossamers.
In a far corner the sun winks,
thinks of a joke not yet said, smiles
back under clouds till the edge silver
is gone. Snow anyway is the language
of any tongue—English snow,
French snow, Russian snow, Polish snow.
When seasons have gone, words white
upon a black landscape, a reverse
of generalities. A white owl watches
a white cat, hair covering troubled
bones, feathers this side of center,
akin to Alute, future garden of white,
book of gentle ice, words already
written. Tracks of all that come and go
mark final punctuation, the melting.

Part III

To Wake a World

30

To Wake a World

To wake a world I sing mostly to that dark
where spread and welcome no sun enters in
and deeper still like rings of ancient trees
each season's circle a judgement
that holds eternity in special glance.

I know all the secret lines of hand and leaves,
where the soul of buried acorns lie.

Lovers, too, worship that awesome dance
the awful nakedness of cloudless sky.

Born then, from the night I will return;
yet willingly I seek the heart of ice.

31

Moment

In the green presence of raindrops
beside time's listening ears
the brown leaves, a winter down,
speak their little voices, whisper
like Eden's forked tongues,
till the day rises in light and song.

The limbs, nude as love, hang heavy
with birds red, black, and blue—
feathers not so quiet as butterflies,
more than crocus about to bloom,
more than grass held still and blond
or stones shedding winter thaw.

The wind an easy pattern shoved by sun,
cloud hidden but warming still, speaks to rain,
the rain to leaves, the leaves to earth.
Buds, about to leaf, look down, down there
in the whispering brown,
down in the sorrow.

White Patch

The white patch of winter thought lies
in the crotch of the tree, the land gone
clear of angels combing hair, and black
limbs grow around the final meeting,
hidden in the way it disappears,
hidden like love working down
to its own roots beginning. It will
come back, not as snow or even love,
but something nurturing in the way
those dark hairs slip silently in soil
searching moment's moisture, time's light.
It will rise even above present wait,
high to limbs and leaves and eyes stare
blankly toward some dangerous distance
fog bound in dream. And there you will know
that awful burden of melting snow.

The Morning Before the Day After

Shaggy the baby robin sits low
in dew leaves, having unnested
where yesterday's last light failed,
that first plunge into life's open air.
Not how far or why or immortal
reasons lost but to fly with still
a too blunted tail to guide. He
sits, contemplating the high limbs,
the brown folded sticks and mud
from which he came. The clouds
are robed for rain, a wetness
more than his first rude soaking
and inside each drop a darkness
deep as the one he's just come through.
Witness, too, how death already stalks
in the high grass, sleek and quiet
as newborn ice, black as the heart's
silence. Step by step and they say
it's nature's way, a reminder
of the universe's brutal scolding
to every child where
tender wings need not remember
because there is no way to forget.

A Wash of Wish

Darkness holds not the bitter turn
so much in stress, fingers twisted light,
to comprehend passion's gift, uphold fire,
where in the wood hide the smoke and heat.

Light burns not the lips kiss of dawn
wise to ways clouds tremble over land
lover water drip down a wash of wish
favored fountains coins in the hand.

Land where feet have gone and silent now
bones of old travelers bound to earth
the second element a prisoner of each
sacred where the moment spills forth.

Leaves

Don't hurt the wisdom of the leaves,
the veiny light catchers bound
and tree held against the wind.
Weep not for such apparent imprisonment
but sing, sing with the birds in merriment
as if the end of every flight is song.
The shade they cast is evidence enough
a willingness to separate, a go between
the heat and cool as if hidden in lizard eyes.
Their gift, if any universe pay homage to truth
unrelative, is themselves returning (or is
it turning?) where they've never been
down, down to earth that other leaves
might bud and go that same flattened way,
change the only constancy anyway.

Wake

I

And so the night wakes remembering—
a dream tasting of tin, metallic as
foil gritted on bare teeth. Distance
no matter. The space of the second
mind like dark holes webbed with
mysterious theories. Every night
new star explodes. Wheel-less
travelers on bleak time roads, a
third sound translates far away
cry, a long ago moan,
echo transversing valley chambers
until gone. Little anyway remembered
past the morning finding its way
along winter yards, the crippled grass
hiding deep in its roots.

II

Hiding deep in its roots
and so the night wakes remembering—
along winter yards, the crippled grass
a dream tasting of tin, metallic as
past the morning finding its way
foil gritted on bare teeth. Distance
until gone. Little anyway remembered
no matter. The space of the second
echo transversing valley chambers
mind like dark holes webbed with
cry, a long ago moan, mysterious
theories. Every night
third sound translates far away
new star explodes. Wheel-less
travelers on bleak time roads.

III

Hiding deep in its roots
along winter yards, the crippled grass
past the morning finding its way
until gone. Little anyway remembered
echo transversing valley chambers
cry, a long ago moan,
third sound translates far away
travelers on bleak time roads,
new star explodes. Wheel-less
mysterious theories. Every night
mind like dark holes webbed with
no matter. The space of the second
foil gritted on bare teeth. Distance
a dream tasting tin, metallic as
And so the night wakes remembering.

Part IV

Circles

Circles

Forgive buds of springs; they know
no better, having hid in winter's womb.
Forget memory's balance of love,
the brown leaves down, the sweeping
icy winds, the rising sap breaking life
open; absolve them their plight.
They know only circles and circles
within, being where they go,
being where they've been. It is the ragged
claw of universe. Every stone
has eyes, and granite carved perfect.
Wisdom can not read.
Forgive the buds; they do not realize.

Plunge of Feathers

How to know the world trembles in freefall
around some seaweed green, tumbling water
the size of the heart splashing ever toward
eyes bound sacred in their stare, a moment
benthonic, enough to hold us even in air,
that the question—a darkness true as wisdom,
light sure as silver, love no little boat
at water's edge but the plunge of feathers
somewhere down from sun, down and down.
In an atmosphere wet with longing
Zeus' bolt both hammer and nail searches
the length of Troy, walls precious as
any horse to hide our grief, and there,
fathoming labyrinth of love, desire's
wings; when we have seen that space
above dreams, no melting need inquire
the sphere's command; we grasp indelible
such promise high above the land.

Thigmotropism

Behind walls heart vines grow
as if in space exempt of eyes
no blindness is, in great circles
clockwise the search for pole
to hold love's weight upright.

Motion first in the wide open air
strangely slipping around the sun,
the moon, with night always
undone where first touch makes aware
spiral climbing upward to the light.

Even before, as eyes across a dark room,
something pole to vine, vine to pole, is said—
sound without sound, wave without wave,
instead life's weaving on that invisible loom
the waft and warp to hold it tight.

We surely, string and stem, hear
that call, a silent vision sight
when at such greening moment
we concentrically upward take flight.

45

Not Enough

There are not enough nights for moons
reflecting willing light, nor candle wicks
and flames to burn, nor, hearts to hold
all the fatal turns of time and love.

There are not enough days for suns
having down bright clouds, nor streams
nor mirrors held and hid in silence
of faces torn, heart splashes sorrow born.

There are not enough ears to hear
the lips that speak, nor dancing universe
cheek to cheek with stars aborning and dying burn,
helpless wisdom, ageless crutches worn.

There are not enough songs to sing
nor words to fill a world music mad
nor hands to wake applause, the singer done,
yet still blood rushes and lyrics are glad.

In a Morning Not Yet Gone

In a morning not yet gone, but light
more than some brief happening, songs
rise above brown grass rested and smoky air,
and I turn on the heart's wheel
where frail feathers lift flight
to singing ones, red and red against the high,
turn with the mind's subtle workings—
a mirage slipped from night and dreams.

Lifted so as if such reckoning make
the wiser wise, born in blue particles
of space, and all the stones are gods—
frost and ice, winter hamartia—
a breaking final as empty glasses.

Dogs, siren disturbed, punctuate the place
stretching like a great sentence
around the neighborhood.

Except the evergreens, all limbs
dark, asleep or dead—no profitable guess
for any distant eyes. Except limbs
whispery as butterflies hiding with the rest—
the dreams, the night, the question songs,
the soft replies, and up where touch goes blind
a crow rewrites the sky.

Music's Sphere

What must you do to earn
the night? Into song
stilled surely as lips of birds
frozen of light
nowhere, not in words,
can silence burn
lifting flames long
beyond the ear
yet noise, constant fear.

What must you do to set
in motion music's sphere—
a turning in a turn
a movement out of quiet?
Wings wave without devotion
to flight; songs clear
lie still as discarded white
snake skins (love's lament).
Precious that loss
and yet no time to forget.

Down To

Near the end of the Moon of the Black Cherries
drops slip down past voice of morning dove
to eyes of grass memory which
crawls, spreads, parts the green. It is
not so easy in the valley of hands
where heart lines hold true, to wake
among shadows of love, to turn with
the sun's burn, listening to the universe hum.
Inside water's stillness laughter licks quiet
faces. Salome trees stand where stallion moans slip
away on wind. What anyway would day be
without night, dust without rain?
Light is little more than dark washed blood, red clean,
only a stone's cry from the nearest soul.

Moon, Nearly Full

At the green tunnel's end the road
leads everywhere and waiting eyes
search the fireflies approach, the devil's
scarlet going near the silence of wood
with only three twigs snapping—a hint
of the heart's belief, evidence of lovers, or
dogs, or something wild, or even a beer can
jumping under wheels passing, passing by.

Darkness grows, rises like hope over mowed lawns
and then high from the horizon breaking
away from soft July clouds, the moon,
two thirds its cycle, mocks moving lights,
a touch of horsemint in the air, shadowy
air, a thought of red the way lovers bloom
startles the mind's screen subtle as leaf veins.

Nearly full, pale yellow flower
soft as pearl in the jade sky,
nearly, nearly, nearly full—and down
here, watching the green tunnel,
listening to snapping wood, on the edge
of nearly, the fourth moment, that
dimension, exactly here, both right,
while sand slips through glass curved
like a woman.

50

Rain

In the distance a soft rumble of thunder
disturbs the silence of morning air,
and feet bare slip across wet green
knowing as lovers know the glad touch
of toes to grass. A pressing cool wind,
the rain's hair, awakes the leaves,
limbs a swirl—a comb for the invisible.
Dreaming this way the pattern of rain,
out of dark clouds the crystal orbs,
sings peach blossoms the color of veins
where the heart reaches into the universe
of thought, water drops made, the eyes
windows caught in the blinds of wondering.
So close, yet so far away; so near, yet impossible.
Night's spirit slips like roots underground
and the fourth dimension holds with here
a mirror for the sky (puddles of our loving)
where we listen to the clap of far-away hands,
remembering the bright lightning.

Pastora Molina

Daughter of Seville,
when you dance, Spain comes
trembling silver on your feet
and eyes, dark with verda mystery,
catch the light, fold it in a stare
looking nowhere,
looking everywhere.

Daughter of Seville,
when you dance, Spain comes
worshipping the night in your hands
with lips of castanets
flinging sound tied to strange listening.

Daughter of Seville,
when you dance, Spain comes
on your dress, your shawl
sweeping the air like fire, like sea—
burning memory on the mind
tumbling sand love grains free.

Daughter of Seville,
when you dance, Spain comes
dreaming in your constant eyes,
love spilling silently from your hands,
full moon on your feet.

The night will never be the same.

Pastora Molina

Hija de Sevilla
cuando tú bailas, España viene
temblando plata a tus pies
y ojos de verde misterio
coge la luz y la abraza en una mirada
mirando a ninguna parte
mirando a todas partes.

Hija de Sevilla
cuando tú bailas, España viene
adorando la noche en tus manos
con labios de castañuelas
lanzando sonido atado a extraño escuchar.

Hija de Sevilla
cuando tú bailas, España viene
en tu vestido, tu chal
barriendo el aire como fuego, como el mar
quemando recuerdos en la mente
volteando arena de amor granos libres.

Hija de Sevilla
cuando tú bailas, España viene
soñando en tus constantes ojos
amor derramándose silenciosamente de tus manos
luna llena a tus pies.

La noche nunca más será lo mismo.

53

Raincrow

The raincrow's coo reminds of rain;
shadows dream puddles on the lawn.

Sun spills through limbs leaf filled;
no wind, even whispers, all stilled.

Feathers scattered—brown and gray—
swirled where catdeath stalked the day.

The coo mournful, surely not for rain,
but a lover who will not again.

54

About the Author

Lee Pennington, a native Kentuckian, grew up in the hill country of Greenup County. He graduated from Berea College and the University of Iowa.

The author of eight previous collections of poetry, he has published in over 300 magazines in America and abroad. His *I Knew a Woman* was nominated for a Pulitzer Prize. In 1984 the State Legislature named him Poet Laureate of Kentucky.

He and his wife, Joy, have traveled widely–all 50 states and 51 foreign countries. They are both professors of English at Jefferson Community College in Louisville. They live in Middletown, Kentucky.

Colophon

Thigmotropism is the first volume of the Green River Writers/Grex Press (11906 Locust Road, Middletown, Kentucky 40243) Poetry Series edited by Mary O'Dell. The book was designed by Ben Ruiz of Power Graphics. Headline type is 20 pt. Caslon Open Face and text is 12 pt. Veljovic Book.

First Edition
of 1450 Copies
400 Bound in Boards
50 Special Edition, Boxed, Signed and Numbered